Bon Appétit

HOMESTYLE COOKING

Hearty Soups

**Bon Appétit
Publishing Corp.
Publisher**

Los Angeles

Published by Bon Appétit Publishing Corp. 5900 Wilshire Boulevard, Los Angeles, California 90036

Printed and bound in the United States of America

On the cover: *Turkey Vegetable Soup*

Photograph by Dick Sharpe

Contents

1

Vegetable Soups

Artichoke Soup Annette

Can also be served cold.

6 to 8 servings

- ¼ cup (½ stick) butter
- 1 medium onion, chopped
- 2 pounds fresh Jerusalem artichokes (sunchokes), cooked, peeled and coarsely chopped
- 5 cups chicken stock
  Salt and freshly ground white pepper
- ½ cup whipping cream
  Chopped fresh parsley (garnish)

Melt butter in medium skillet over medium heat. Add onion

and sauté until translucent, about 10 minutes. Puree onion and artichokes in batches with some of stock in blender or processor. Pour into 3-quart saucepan. Blend in remaining stock. Simmer until heated through, about 15 minutes. Season to taste with salt and white pepper. Ladle into bowls. Stir about 1 tablespoon cream into center of each serving, combining just enough to show swirl of cream. Garnish with fresh parsley.

Cream of Artichoke Soup

4 servings

- ½ cup plus 2 tablespoons (1¼ sticks) unsalted butter
- ½ cup chopped carrot
- ½ cup chopped celery
- ½ cup chopped onion
- ½ cup chopped mushrooms

- ¼ cup unbleached all purpose flour
- 1 cup chicken stock
- 2 8½-ounce cans (drained weight) quartered

artichoke hearts, juice
reserved
1 bay leaf
¾ teaspoon salt
½ teaspoon freshly ground
pepper
¼ teaspoon cayenne
pepper
¼ teaspoon dried thyme,
crumbled or ¾ teaspoon
minced fresh
¼ teaspoon dried oregano,
crumbled or ¾ teaspoon
minced fresh
¼ teaspoon sage
Pinch of Hungarian
sweet paprika

1 cup whipping cream

Melt 2 tablespoons butter in
large heavy skillet over medium
heat. Add carrot, celery, onion
and mushrooms and sauté until
vegetables are soft and onion is
translucent, about 15 minutes.

Melt remaining butter in large
stockpot over low heat. Add flour
and cook, stirring constantly, 5
minutes. Stir in vegetables. Add
stock in slow steady stream, stirring constantly. Add artichoke
hearts with juice, bay leaf, salt,
pepper, cayenne pepper, thyme,

oregano, sage and paprika and stir through. Increase heat to medium and simmer 30 minutes, stirring occasionally.

Beat cream in small bowl just until frothy. Blend into soup. Heat through; do not boil. Adjust seasoning and serve.

Asparagus Soup

4 to 6 servings

> 1 to 2 tablespoons butter
> 4 to 5 escarole leaves, shredded
> 1 pound thin asparagus, trimmed and cut diagonally into ¼-inch pieces
> 6 cups rich chicken stock, at boiling point
>   Salt and freshly ground pepper
> 2 whole green onions, minced
>   Freshly grated Parmesan cheese

Heat butter in skillet over medium-high heat. Add escarole and asparagus and sauté 2 minutes. Add to stock, increase heat to high and boil just until asparagus is crisp-tender. Season to taste with salt and pepper. Sprinkle each serving with green onion and pass freshly grated Parmesan cheese.

To vary for a richer soup: Combine 3 egg yolks with ½ cup whipping cream. After soup has cooked, remove from heat and slowly beat 1 cup stock into yolk mixture. Return to saucepan and stir constantly over low heat several minutes until slightly thickened. (Do not let soup boil or yolks will curdle.) Pour into heated bowls and serve.

Maria Luna's Black Bean Soup

12 servings

  1 pound dried black beans
1½ tablespoons salt
  ¼ teaspoon freshly ground pepper
   Large bouquet garni (large bay leaf, 2 fresh thyme sprigs, 4 fresh parsley sprigs)
   Pinch of dried oregano, crumbled

1½ cups chicken stock
(preferably homemade)

½ cup (1 stick) butter
1 cup sliced green onion
2 medium Anaheim
chilies, split and seeded
2 medium garlic cloves,
minced
1 cup dry vermouth
Lemon slices (garnish)

Soak beans in cold water to cover
at least 8 hours or overnight.
Discard any that float. Drain
beans and combine with 4
quarts water in stockpot. Bring
to boil over high heat, skimming
foam from surface. Add salt,
pepper, bouquet garni and dried
oregano. Reduce heat, cover and
cook until beans are tender,
about 3 hours, skimming foam
from surface if necessary.

Strain off bean cooking liquid
and reserve. Remove bouquet
garni. Puree beans in processor
or blender. Transfer to heavy
large saucepan. Blend in stock
and enough bean cooking liquid
(about half) to achieve medium-
thick consistency.

Melt butter in heavy medium skillet over medium-low heat. Add green onion, chilies and garlic and cook until tender, stirring occasionally, about 15 minutes. Add to soup. Blend dry vermouth into soup. Cook over medium-low heat 15 minutes, adding more reserved bean cooking liquid if thinner consistency is desired. Season with salt and pepper. Ladle soup into bowls. Garnish with lemon slices and serve.

Cream of Carrot Soup

Makes about 4 cups

- 2 tablespoons (¼ stick) butter
- 6 green onions (including green tops), chopped
- 4 large carrots, sliced
- 1 or 2 large celery stalks, sliced
- 2 cups rich chicken stock
- ½ cup whipping cream or half and half
  Salt and freshly ground white pepper
  Chopped parsley (garnish)

Melt butter in large saucepan over high heat. Add onion, carrot and celery and stir to coat. Blend in chicken stock. Bring to boil over high heat. Reduce heat to medium, cover and simmer until vegetables are soft, about 30 minutes. Transfer mixture to blender and puree. Return to pan. Add cream, salt and pepper and stir over low heat until warmed through; do not boil. Ladle into bowls and sprinkle with parsley. Serve immediately.

Celery Root Soup

Accompany with French bread and sweet butter.

8 servings

- ¼ cup (½ stick) unsalted butter
- 1 large leek, trimmed and thinly sliced
- 6 to 8 cups chicken stock
- 3 large celery roots, peeled and cubed
- 2 medium potatoes, peeled and cubed
- 1 parsnip, peeled and cubed

1 cup whipping cream
Salt and freshly ground
white pepper
Minced fresh parsley
(garnish)

Heat butter in large heavy saucepan or Dutch oven over medium heat. Add leek, cover and cook until leek is tender but not browned, 3 to 4 minutes. Pour in stock and add remaining vegetables. Bring to boil, then reduce heat, cover and simmer until vegetables are tender, about 45 to 60 minutes. Allow to cool.

Transfer in batches to blender or processor and puree; strain. Return to saucepan and stir in cream and salt and pepper to taste. Bring to serving temperature, taste and adjust seasonings. Ladle into individual bowls and garnish with parsley.

Eggplant Soup au Gratin

8 servings

- 2 tablespoons olive oil
- 1 medium onion, sliced
- 2 garlic cloves, minced
- 2 medium or large eggplants, peeled and cubed
- 1 teaspoon dried oregano
- ½ teaspoon dried thyme
- 4 cups chicken stock
- ½ cup Sherry
  Salt and freshly ground pepper

- 2 tomatoes, sliced
- 1½ cups grated Swiss cheese
  Freshly grated Parmesan cheese

Heat oil in large kettle or Dutch oven over medium-high heat. Add onion and garlic and sauté until onion is transparent. Add eggplant, oregano and thyme and sauté 2 minutes. Blend in stock, reduce heat, cover and simmer 20 minutes. Add Sherry and continue simmering 3 minutes more. Add salt and pepper to taste. *(Can be prepared ahead to this point and refrigerated.)*

Preheat broiler. Pour soup into ovenproof bowls. Top soup with tomato slices and cheeses. Broil until cheese is melted and lightly browned, about 2 minutes. Serve immediately.

Turkish Lentil Soup

6 to 8 servings

    1 cup dried lentils
    3 cups beef stock
    2 tablespoons chopped fresh parsley

    3 tablespoons butter
    1 large onion, finely chopped
    3 cups tomato juice
       Dash of cayenne pepper
       Additional stock *or* tomato juice (optional)
       Salt and freshly ground pepper (optional)

Combine lentils, stock and parsley in medium saucepan. Bring to boil. Reduce heat, cover and simmer until lentils are tender, about 30 minutes, stirring occasionally.

Melt butter in large saucepan over medium heat. Add onion

and sauté until golden. Stir in
lentils and stock, tomato juice
and cayenne. Cover and simmer
30 minutes. If too thick, stir in
additional stock or tomato juice.
Taste and adjust seasoning with
salt and pepper and additional
cayenne if desired.

Onion Soup with Cheese Croutons

4 to 6 servings

- ¼ cup (½ stick) butter
- 4 large yellow onions, thinly sliced
- ½ teaspoon sugar
- 6 cups beef stock
- 1 teaspoon Worcestershire sauce
- ½ teaspoon paprika
  Salt and freshly ground pepper

- 4 to 6 slices French bread
  Butter
- ¼ cup (about) freshly grated Gruyère *or* Parmesan cheese

Heat butter in large saucepan
over medium heat. Add onion
and sugar and sauté until

golden. Add stock, Worcestershire and paprika and bring to boil. Reduce heat and simmer uncovered 15 to 20 minutes. Add salt and pepper.

Meanwhile, toast bread on one side under broiler. Spread untoasted side with butter and sprinkle with cheese. Return to broiler until lightly toasted. Ladle soup into bowls and float toast. (If soup bowls are ovenproof, float bread and run under broiler to toast second side.)

Quick Potage Saint-Germain

The foundation of this recipe is an enriched canned chicken stock. This same technique can be used with beef stock.

6 servings

2 13½-ounce cans chicken stock
1 onion, chopped
1 celery stalk with leaves
1 small carrot, chopped

2 10-ounce packages frozen tiny peas, thawed

2 small green onions,
  chopped
¼ teaspoon minced garlic
1 cup whipping cream
  Salt and freshly ground
  white pepper

Combine stock, onion, celery and carrot in saucepan. Cover and simmer 30 to 45 minutes.

Add peas, green onions and garlic. Cover and simmer 5 minutes. Transfer to blender in batches and puree until smooth. Turn into saucepan, blend in cream and heat through. Season with salt and pepper. Serve hot or chilled. *(Can be made up to 2 days ahead and refrigerated.)*

Spicy Pumpkin Soup

Makes about 1 quart

- 2 tablespoons (¼ stick) butter
- 2 celery stalks, diced
- 1 onion, chopped
- 1 tablespoon all purpose flour
- 1 teaspoon salt
- ⅛ teaspoon ground ginger
- ⅛ teaspoon freshly grated nutmeg
- 3 cups chicken stock
- 1½ pounds diced pumpkin or 1 16-ounce can
- 1 cup half and half *or* milk
  Chopped green onion (garnish)

Melt butter in large saucepan over medium heat. Add celery and onion and sauté until onion is golden, about 10 minutes. Blend in flour, salt, ginger and nutmeg and cook 3 minutes. Stir in chicken stock and pumpkin. Simmer mixture for 30 minutes. Transfer to processor (in batches if necessary) and puree until smooth. Turn into large bowl. Stir in half and half, blending well. Ladle soup into bowls. Garnish with green onion and serve.

Italian Tomato and Red Pepper Soup

12 servings

- 2 tablespoons (¼ stick) unsalted butter
- 1 tablespoon olive oil
- 3 large onions, thinly sliced
- 6 large red bell peppers, seeded and thinly sliced
- 6 large garlic cloves
- 1 large carrot, diced
- ½ teaspoon dried thyme
- ½ teaspoon dried oregano
  Bouquet garni (bay leaf, celery leaves, leek greens, parsley sprigs, 2-inch strip of orange peel tied in cheesecloth bag)
  Salt
  Cayenne pepper

- 12 large ripe tomatoes, peeled, seeded and chopped *or* 6 cups peeled canned tomatoes, drained and chopped
- 3 tablespoons dry Sherry
- 1 tablespoon red wine vinegar

5 cups defatted chicken
  stock
  Freshly ground pepper

Puree Saint-Germain*

Melt butter with oil in large non-aluminum saucepan over medium heat. Add onion and cook until just golden (do not brown). Add next 8 ingredients and blend well. Reduce heat to low, cover and cook 10 minutes, stirring several times.

Add tomatoes, Sherry and vinegar and cook uncovered, stirring frequently, 10 minutes. Stir in stock. Bring to boil, reduce heat and simmer 10 minutes. Season to taste with pepper.

Discard bouquet garni, pressing out any cooking liquid into soup. Set large sieve over bowl and strain soup, pressing vegetables through sieve with back of spoon. Return to saucepan and heat. To serve, swirl several spoonfuls of Puree Saint-Germain through each portion, or pass puree separately.

*Puree Saint-Germain

Makes about 3½ to 4 cups

- 4 cups fresh peas *or* frozen green peas, thawed
- 4 green onions, thinly sliced
- ½ to 1 cup whipping cream Salt and freshly ground pepper

In medium saucepan, cook peas and onion in boiling salted water just until tender. Drain, refresh under cold water and drain again. Transfer to processor or blender, add ½ cup cream and puree. Thin with additional cream until same consistency as soup. Season with salt and pepper. Serve hot.

dagdart

Spinach-Rice Soup

4 to 6 servings

    4 to 4½ cups chicken stock
    1½ cups cooked rice
    1 10-ounce package frozen
       chopped spinach,
       thawed
       Freshly ground pepper
       Finely grated cheddar or
       Monterey Jack cheese
       (garnish)

Combine 4 cups chicken stock with rice and spinach in 2-quart saucepan over medium-high heat and cook until heated through. Season with pepper. Add more stock if thinner consistency is desired. Ladle into bowls. Garnish with cheese. Serve immediately.

Cream of Vegetable Soup Normandy

6 servings

    ¼ cup (½ stick) butter
    6 medium carrots, thinly
       sliced
    3 large leeks, cleaned and
       thinly sliced (include
       1-inch green stem)

2 large onions, thinly
  sliced
2 large turnips, peeled and
  thinly sliced
6 potatoes, peeled and
  sliced
8 cups chicken stock
  Salt and freshly ground
  pepper
1 cup Crème Fraîche*

Melt butter in Dutch oven or large saucepan over medium heat. Add carrot, leeks, onion and turnips and sauté until golden. Add potatoes, stock and salt (if necessary) and pepper to taste. Increase heat and bring to boil. Reduce heat and simmer until vegetables are tender. Transfer to processor or blender in batches and puree. Return to saucepan and stir in Crème Fraîche. Cook over low heat until just warmed through (do not boil). Serve immediately.

*Crème Fraîche

Makes 1 cup

1 cup whipping cream
1 tablespoon buttermilk

Combine cream and buttermilk

in jar with tight-fitting lid and shake briskly 1 minute. Let stand at room temperature overnight until thickened. Shake again. Refrigerate until ready to use.

Curried Cream of Vegetable Soup

4 to 6 servings

      3 carrots, chopped
     ½ head cauliflower, chopped
      1 medium onion, chopped
      1 medium potato, peeled and chopped
      1 tablespoon chopped fresh parsley
      2 chicken bouillon cubes
      1 cup whipping cream
     ½ teaspoon curry powder
     ¼ teaspoon Worcestershire sauce
         Freshly ground white pepper

Bring 3 cups water to boil in 2-quart saucepan over medium-high heat. Add carrot, cauliflower, onion, potato, parsley and bouillon cubes and return to boil. Continue cooking until vegetables are tender, about 15 minutes. Transfer mixture to blender or processor in batches and puree until smooth. Return to saucepan. Blend in whipping cream. Mix in remaining ingredients. Place over medium heat and cook until heated through. Ladle into bowls. Serve hot.

Tuscan Peasant Soup

6 servings

 ¼ cup olive oil
 3 large onions, sliced
 ½ pound red bell peppers *or* green bell peppers (or combination), cut into strips
 1½ pounds tomatoes, peeled and chopped
 1 cup diced celery

 12 slices Italian bread, cut ½ inch thick
 1 small garlic clove
 2 tablespoons olive oil

 4 cups chicken stock, at boiling point
 1 tablespoon tomato paste (optional)
 4 eggs

¾ cup freshly grated
  Parmesan cheese
  Salt and freshly ground
  pepper

Heat ¼ cup oil in large saucepan over medium-high heat. Add onion and sauté until lightly browned. Add peppers and continue sautéing until vegetables are well browned. Blend in tomatoes and celery and cook briskly, stirring frequently, about 30 minutes.

Meanwhile, brush each slice of bread with mixture of garlic mashed with 2 tablespoons olive oil. Run under broiler until toasted on both sides. Place 2 slices in each soup plate.

Add stock to vegetables and let boil 5 minutes. Stir in tomato paste (this will enhance color). Beat eggs and cheese together. Whisking soup constantly, quickly add egg-cheese mixture. Season to taste with salt and pepper. Ladle soup over toast and serve immediately.

Minestrone with Winter Pesto Sauce

A light vegetable puree thickens the broth, making it richer and more nutritious.

Makes about 12 cups

½ cup dried navy beans, rinsed and sorted

4 large garlic cloves
4 medium onions, quartered
3 medium celery stalks, peeled and cut into 1-inch pieces
1 medium potato, peeled and quartered
2 tablespoons olive oil
5½ cups beef broth
2 medium tomatoes, peeled, seeded and quartered

6 tablespoons tomato paste

3 medium carrots, cut into 2-inch lengths
8 ounces fresh green beans, cut into 1½-inch lengths

2 small zucchini, cut into
   feed tube lengths
2 teaspoons salt
   Freshly ground pepper

Winter Pesto Sauce*

Place navy beans in bowl and
cover completely with cold
water. Let soak overnight.

Drain beans. Transfer to large
saucepan. Cover generously
with water and bring to boil over
medium-high heat. Reduce heat
and simmer 20 minutes. Drain
beans well and set aside.

With processor machine running, drop garlic through feed
tube and mince finely. Add onions, celery and potato to work
bowl and mince. Heat olive oil
in 6- to 8-quart saucepan over
low heat. Add onion mixture. Set
piece of waxed paper directly
atop vegetables and cook 15
minutes, stirring occasionally;
do not let vegetables brown. Discard waxed paper. Add 1½ cups
broth to vegetables. Cover and
cook over medium heat until all
vegetables are soft, about 30
minutes. Place tomatoes in work
bowl and chop coarsely using

several on/off turns. Remove from work bowl and set aside.

Strain onion mixture, returning liquid to saucepan. Transfer vegetables to processor and puree 1 minute, stopping to scrape down sides of work bowl. Stir vegetable puree back into saucepan. Add cooked beans, remaining 4 cups beef broth, chopped tomatoes and tomato paste and blend well.

Insert slicer in processor. Stand carrots in feed tube and slice using firm pressure. Add to soup. Place saucepan over medium heat and cook 15 minutes. Stack green beans in feed tube horizontally and slice using light pressure. Remove from work bowl and set aside.

Insert french fry disc in processor. Stand zucchini in feed tube and process using medium pressure. Add green beans and salt and pepper to soup and cook over medium heat 5 minutes. Add zucchini and cook just until all vegetables are crisp-tender, about 5 more minutes. Taste and adjust seasoning. Serve with Winter Pesto Sauce.

*Winter Pesto Sauce

Makes 1½ to 1¾ cups

- 2 large garlic cloves
- 3 ounces Parmesan cheese (preferably imported), room temperature, cut into 3 pieces
- 2 cups tightly packed stemmed spinach leaves *or* Italian parsley, rinsed and dried
- ½ cup pine nuts or walnuts
- 2 tablespoons dried basil
- 1 teaspoon salt
- 1 cup vegetable oil

With processor machine running, drop garlic through feed tube and mince finely. Add cheese and chop using 4 on/off turns, then process until finely minced, about 1 minute. Add spinach, nuts, basil and salt and blend 10 seconds. With machine running, pour oil through feed tube in slow, steady stream and blend well. Transfer to small bowl and serve immediately.

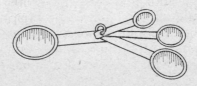

Vegetable-Cheese Chowder

4 servings

2½ cups water
2 cups diced peeled
  potatoes
¾ cup minced leeks
½ cup diced celery
2½ teaspoons salt

¼ cup (½ stick) butter
¼ cup all purpose flour
2 cups milk
1½ teaspoons
  Worcestershire sauce
½ teaspoon dry mustard
¼ teaspoon freshly ground
  pepper
1 12-ounce can cubed
  tomatoes, drained
4 ounces freshly grated
  Parmesan cheese
1 tablespoon minced fresh
  parsley

Bring water to boil in large saucepan over high heat. Add potatoes, leeks, celery and 1 teaspoon salt. Return to boil. Reduce heat to medium-low, cover and simmer until vegetables are tender, about 15 minutes.

Melt butter in medium saucepan over medium-low heat. Remove from heat and blend in flour. Add milk, Worcestershire sauce, remaining 1½ teaspoons salt, mustard and pepper. Return to medium-low heat and stir until thickened, about 10 minutes. Stir into potato mixture. Add tomatoes, Parmesan and parsley. Ladle soup into heated bowls and serve.

Cheese Soup

6 servings

- 1 small onion, coarsely chopped
- 1 small green bell pepper, coarsely chopped
- 2 celery stalks, cut into small pieces
- 2 carrots, cut into small pieces
- ¼ cup (½ stick) butter
- ¼ cup all purpose flour
- 3½ cups chicken stock
- 3 cups grated cheddar cheese
- 1½ cups milk
- 2 tablespoons Sherry

Salt and freshly ground
pepper
Minced fresh parsley
(garnish)
Beer, room temperature

Combine first 4 ingredients in
processor or blender and finely
chop. Melt butter in 3-quart
saucepan over medium heat.
Add vegetables and cook 8 to 10
minutes, stirring occasionally.
Add flour and stir until well
blended. Pour in chicken stock
and bring to boil, stirring constantly, until soup is slightly
thickened. Remove from heat.
Add cheese and allow to melt.
Add milk, Sherry and salt and
pepper to taste and mix thoroughly. Ladle into heated mugs
and sprinkle with parsley. Top
with small amount of beer before serving if desired.

Seafood Soups

Crab and Vegetable Soup

Makes about 5 quarts

> 1 pound flanken, top rib
> or beef ribs
> ½ pound soup bones
> 10 to 11 cups water
> 1 large onion, chopped
> 2 celery stalks, diced
> 3 carrots, diced
> ½ cup baby lima beans,
> rinsed
> ¼ cup split peas
> ¼ cup barley
> 1½ large potatoes, peeled
> and diced
> 1½ zucchini, diced
> ¾ cup string beans, broken
> into thirds

> 1 3-ounce can corn, drained
> 2½ ounces frozen peas
> 3 tomatoes, chopped *or* 1 14-ounce can tomatoes, drained (reserve juice)
> 3 beef bouillon cubes
> 1 teaspoon Old Bay seafood seasoning
> 1 teaspoon salt
> ½ teaspoon freshly ground pepper
>
> 6 ounces fresh or frozen crabmeat

Rinse beef ribs and transfer to large, heavy stockpot. Add bones and 6 cups water. Bring to boil over high heat, skimming foam from surface as necessary. Reduce heat to medium-high. Add onion and celery and cook 15 minutes, skimming foam from surface again if necessary. Add carrot, lima beans, split peas and barley and continue cooking on medium-high heat 20 minutes. Skim again if necessary. Add potato, zucchini, string beans, corn and peas. Stir in remaining 4 to 5 cups water, depending on desired thickness. Continue cooking on medium-high heat 30 minutes. Add tomatoes and juice, bouillon, seafood seasoning, salt and pepper. Reduce heat to low and cook, stirring occasionally, until vegetables are tender, about 30 minutes.

Discard soup bones. Remove beef ribs and let cool. Cut meat from ribs and return to soup. Add crabmeat and heat just until cooked through (or warmed through if frozen), about 2 to 3 minutes. Taste and adjust seasoning. Serve immediately.

Bay Scallop Soup

4 servings

- 2 8-ounce bottles clam juice
- 1 tablespoon unsalted butter
- ½ teaspoon Worcestershire sauce
- ½ teaspoon dry mustard
- ⅛ teaspoon garlic powder
- ⅛ teaspoon celery salt
- ¾ pound bay scallops
- 2 egg yolks
- 1 cup whipping cream
  Snipped fresh chives

Combine first 6 ingredients in medium saucepan and bring to boil. Add scallops and simmer gently 3 minutes. Beat yolks with cream in bowl. Ladle about ½ cup hot soup into cream and blend well. Gradually stir cream mixture back into soup. Stir until soup thickens slightly, 1 to 2 minutes. Sprinkle with chives. Serve immediately.

Lobster Pot Soup

8 servings

    3 tablespoons butter
    2 onions, thinly sliced
    1 garlic clove, chopped
    2 quarts (or more) beef stock
    1 8-ounce package small shell macaroni
    1 1-pound can whole tomatoes, chopped (reserve liquid)
    1 large bunch spinach, coarsely chopped *or* 1 10-ounce package frozen chopped spinach, thawed
    1 8- to 10-ounce package frozen lobster tails,

thawed and chopped
1 bay leaf
½ teaspoon dried basil,
crumbled
Cayenne pepper

Melt butter in heavy large saucepan over medium-high heat.
Add onion and garlic, cover and
cook until onion is translucent,
about 7 minutes. Pour in 2 quarts
stock and bring to boil. Add
macaroni and cook 5 minutes,
stirring frequently. Stir in tomatoes and liquid, spinach, lob-
ster, bay leaf, basil and cayenne
pepper. Cover and simmer until
macaroni is tender, about 8 minutes. Add more broth if thinner
consistency is desired. Ladle
into bowls and serve hot.

Cheryl Fisher

Quarter-Hour Soup

6 servings

- 2 tablespoons olive oil
- 1 onion, finely chopped
- ¼ pound ham, finely chopped
- ¼ pound uncooked shrimp, shelled and deveined
- ¼ cup blanched almonds, finely ground
- 3 tomatoes, peeled and chopped
- 6 cups chicken stock
- 2 6½-ounce cans minced clams, undrained
- 1 cup freshly cooked rice
- ½ cup fresh peas *or* frozen peas
- 2 hard-cooked eggs, minced (garnish)

Heat oil in large saucepan over medium heat. Add onion and sauté until tender but not browned. Add ham, shrimp and almonds and cook until shrimp turn pink. Remove shrimp; chop and set aside. Add tomatoes to pan and blend well. Stir in stock and undrained clams and bring to boil. Add rice and peas and

simmer 5 minutes. Add shrimp
and cook 1 minute longer. Garnish with minced egg.

Quick Manhattan-style Chowder

Serve with crisp buttered
rye toast.

6 to 8 servings

- ¼ pound bacon, diced
- 1 large garlic clove, minced
- 1 onion, chopped
- 1 green bell pepper, seeded and chopped
- 2 cups chicken stock
- 1 28-ounce can stewed tomatoes
- 2 8-ounce cans minced clams, undrained
- 1 10-ounce can baby clams, undrained
- ½ cup barley
  Tomato juice (optional)
  Salt and freshly ground pepper
  Hot pepper sauce

Brown bacon with garlic in
heavy-bottomed large saucepan

or Dutch oven over medium-high heat. When bacon is almost crisp, add onion and green pepper and sauté until tender. Stir in stock and tomatoes. Add clams and barley and blend well. Bring mixture to boil, reduce heat and simmer to desired thickness, about 20 to 30 minutes. Add tomato juice to thin. Season to taste with salt and pepper and hot pepper sauce.

Spicy Sausage and Clam Soup

Serve with hot, crusty bread.

6 to 8 servings

- ¼ cup olive oil
- 1 pound hot Italian sausage, casings removed
- 1 pound mushrooms, coarsely chopped
- 2 cups sliced onion
- 1 28-ounce can whole peeled Italian tomatoes, undrained
- 1 cup dry white wine
- 1 cup fresh *or* bottled clam juice

2 tablespoons fresh basil
  or 2 teaspoons dried,
  crumbled
1 tablespoon minced garlic

1 large bunch parsley,
  chopped
6 dozen littleneck clams,
  scrubbed

Heat olive oil in large Dutch oven or flameproof casserole over medium heat. Add sausage, mushrooms and onion and cook, stirring frequently and breaking up sausage with fork until sausage loses pink color, about 10 minutes. Stir in tomatoes. Bring mixture to boil, crushing tomatoes into small pieces. Reduce heat to low and simmer 5 minutes. Pour in wine and clam juice. Return mixture to boil. Reduce heat to low, cover and simmer 20 minutes, stirring occasionally. Add basil and garlic and cook 5 minutes longer. *(Stock can be prepared 1 day ahead to this point, covered and refrigerated until ready to use.)*

Before serving, transfer stock to pot large enough to accommodate stock and clams. Bring to boil over high heat. Reserve half of parsley for garnish and add remaining parsley to pot. Add clams. Reduce heat to medium-high, cover and simmer until clams open, about 5 to 10 minutes. Discard any clams that do not open. Ladle soup into bowls and sprinkle with reserved parsley. Serve immediately.

Ten-Minute Tuna Chowder

4 servings

- 2 tablespoons vegetable oil
- ¼ cup chopped green onion
- ½ 6½- or 7-ounce can albacore *or* light tuna, drained
- ¼ teaspoon dried oregano
- ¼ teaspoon dried basil
- 2 cups vegetable stock *or* clam juice
- ½ cup coarsely grated carrot
- ½ cup coarsely grated potato
- ½ cup milk, half and half *or* cottage cheese
  Salt and freshly ground pepper

Heat oil in medium saucepan. Add onion and sauté 2 to 3 minutes. Add tuna and herbs and stir 1 to 2 minutes. Blend in stock or clam juice, carrot and potato. Cover and simmer until vegetables are cooked, 5 to 6 minutes. Remove from heat and add milk, half and half or cottage cheese. (If using cottage cheese, first blend slowly with ½ cup hot stock.) Add salt and pepper to taste. Serve immediately.

Oyster Soup

4 servings

  6 tablespoons olive oil
  4 slices French bread
  1 large garlic clove, mashed

  2 8-ounce jars oysters, undrained
  1 8-ounce bottle clam juice
  ¾ cup red wine
  1 tablespoon catsup
  ½ teaspoon dried oregano
  ½ teaspoon garlic salt
  ¼ teaspoon freshly ground pepper
  2 tablespoons chopped fresh parsley (garnish)

Heat 3 tablespoons olive oil in large saucepan over medium heat. Add bread and brown on both sides. Remove and set aside. Add remaining oil and garlic and cook 2 to 3 minutes to season oil and pan. Remove and discard garlic.

Add all remaining ingredients except parsley and bring to boil. Reduce heat and simmer 10 minutes. Place slice of bread in each bowl and ladle soup over. Garnish with chopped parsley.

Hot and Sour Seafood Soup

6 servings

- 8 cups water
- 1 leek, well rinsed and coarsely chopped
- 3 tablespoons dried lemongrass (citronella)* (optional)
- 4 to 5 slices fresh ginger, unpeeled
- 2 pounds (about) fish trimmings (snapper, bass *or* cod)

*Available at oriental markets.

½ pound uncooked small shrimp, shelled, deveined and halved lengthwise

1 small cucumber, peeled, halved lengthwise, seeded and cut into ¼-inch crescents

4 to 6 tablespoons fish sauce (nuoc mam)*

2 2-inch-square tofu cakes, rinsed and cut into small cubes

½ fresh small hot chili (or to taste), seeded and cut into fine slivers

3 to 4 tablespoons fresh lime juice

3 to 4 tablespoons finely minced cilantro

2 to 3 green onions (green part only), thinly sliced

Combine water, leek, lemongrass and ginger in large saucepan and bring to boil over medium-high heat. Cover partially and let boil 5 minutes. Add fish trimmings. Reduce heat, cover partially and keep at low simmer for 30 minutes. Strain

*Available at oriental markets.

into bowl, adding any bits of fish to broth. Discard bones.

Rinse saucepan. Add broth, shrimp, cucumber, 4 tablespoons fish sauce, tofu and chili. Place over very low heat and keep just under simmer 4 minutes. Stir in 3 tablespoons lime juice. Taste and adjust seasoning with remaining fish sauce and lime juice. Divide cilantro and green onion among bowls. Ladle soup over and serve.

Beggar's Bouillabaisse

6 to 8 servings

- 2 16-ounce cans stewed tomatoes
- 2 8-ounce cans tomato sauce
- 2 medium potatoes, peeled and cut into 1-inch cubes
- 2 onions, coarsely chopped
- 2 green bell peppers, seeded and diced
- 2 garlic cloves, minced
- 1 bay leaf

⅓ cup minced fresh
parsley
1 teaspoon Italian herb
seasoning
1 teaspoon salt
½ teaspoon freshly ground
white pepper
2½ pounds red snapper
fillets *or* fillets of any
firm-fleshed fish, cut
into large pieces
½ pound cooked small to
medium shrimp
1 6½-ounce can chopped
clams, undrained

Combine first 11 ingredients in 3-quart saucepan and bring to boil over medium-high heat. Reduce heat, cover and simmer until vegetables are almost tender, about 30 minutes. Add snapper, shrimp and clams and continue simmering until fish flakes easily with fork, about 10 minutes. Taste and adjust seasoning before serving.

Soupe de Poissons

8 servings

- ½ cup olive oil
- 3 large yellow onions, chopped
- 1 cup chopped leek
- 4 garlic cloves, chopped
- 1½ pounds tomatoes, peeled and chopped
  Bouquet garni (2 sprigs celery leaves, 2 sprigs dried fennel or 1 teaspoon fennel seed, 2 to 3 sprigs fresh thyme or 1 teaspoon dried, 1 tablespoon fresh basil or 1 teaspoon dried, 1 bay leaf, ½ teaspoon grated orange peel)
- 3 to 3½ pounds firm fresh fish, cut into chunks
- 6 cups boiling water
- 2 8-ounce bottles clam juice
- 2 cups dry white wine
  Salt and freshly ground pepper

- ½ teaspoon ground saffron
- 8 slices dried French bread, rubbed with garlic

½ cup (or more) freshly
    grated Parmesan cheese
    Rouille*

Heat olive oil in large Dutch oven
or stockpot over low heat. Add
onion, leek and garlic. Top with
round of waxed paper or parch-
ment. Cover and cook, stirring
occasionally, until vegetables are
soft and transparent, about 15
to 20 minutes (do not brown).
Increase heat to high. Add tomatoes and bouquet garni. Add
fish and cook, stirring constantly, 10 minutes. Add boiling
water, clam juice, wine and salt
and pepper. Cover partially, reduce heat to medium and cook
25 to 30 minutes.

Strain stock into large bowl,
pressing ingredients with back
of wooden spoon to extract as
much liquid as possible. Discard fish, vegetables and bouquet garni. Bring broth to gentle
boil over medium heat. Add saffron and salt and pepper to taste.
Ladle into individual bowls. Top
each serving with bread slice
and sprinkle with Parmesan.
Pass Rouille separately.

*Rouille

Makes 1¼ cups

- 2 small dried red chilies, stemmed
- 1 small bunch basil leaves (optional)
- 2 to 3 garlic cloves
  Coarse salt and freshly ground pepper
- 1 thick slice French bread, soaked in water and squeezed dry
- 1 red bell pepper, broiled, skinned, seeded and ribs removed (optional)
- ½ to ¾ cup olive oil

Crush dried chilies in large mortar until powdered. Add basil, garlic and salt and pepper and blend to paste. Add bread, red bell pepper and continue blending until pureed. Add ½ cup oil in slow steady stream, stirring constantly with pestle until mixture is consistency of mayonnaise and adding more olive oil as necessary.

Regal Fish and Shellfish

4 servings

- 1 medium onion, diced
- 1 cup diced leek
- ½ cup diced celery
- 6 tablespoons (¾ stick) butter
- 2 8-ounce bottles clam juice
- 2 cups dry white wine
- 2 garlic cloves, minced
- 1 bay leaf
- ½ teaspoon dried thyme
- ¼ teaspoon freshly ground pepper
  Generous dash of hot pepper sauce
- ⅓ cup finely chopped fresh parsley

- 12 hard-shell clams, scrubbed
- 1 pound red snapper *or* other rockfish fillets *or* sea bass fillets, cut into 1½-inch squares
- ¾ pound sole fillets, cut into 2½-inch squares
- 12 uncooked medium shrimp, shelled and deveined

1 cup whipping cream, scalded
 Buttered Croutons*
 (garnish)
 Freshly ground white pepper

In large kettle or Dutch oven over medium heat, sauté onion, leek and celery in butter until very tender. Add clam juice (avoid any dark sediment), wine, garlic, bay leaf, thyme, pepper, hot pepper sauce and ¼ cup parsley. Heat to boiling, then simmer uncovered 5 minutes.

Add clams in shells and simmer 5 minutes. Add snapper and simmer 3 minutes. Stir in sole and shrimp and simmer 3 minutes more, or until shrimp are pink, clams are open and fish flesh barely separates when tested with dinner knife. Remove bay leaf. Stir in cream. Ladle into shallow soup plates, arranging shrimp on top. Sprinkle with remaining parsley. Serve with croutons and freshly ground white pepper.

*To Make Buttered Croutons

Slice a French baguette or other slender loaf of French-style bread or French or Italian rolls into slices less than ¼ inch thick. In large frying pan over medium heat, sauté bread in generous amount of butter until golden brown on both sides. Drain thoroughly on paper towels.

Southern Seafood Gumbo

Makes about 3 quarts

- ½ cup bacon drippings
- ½ cup all purpose flour
- 2½ cups chopped onion
- 1½ cups chopped celery
- ¾ cup chopped green onion
- ½ cup chopped green bell pepper
- ¼ cup chopped fresh parsley
- 2 medium garlic cloves, minced

- 1 quart chicken stock
- 2 cups water
- 2 cups dry white wine
- 1 14½-ounce can tomatoes, drained and chopped
- ¼ cup catsup
- 1 bay leaf
- ¾ teaspoon filé powder

½ teaspoon salt

½ teaspoon chopped fresh
chervil

⅛ teaspoon dried thyme,
crumbled

⅛ dried rosemary,
crumbled

⅛ teaspoon dried oregano,
crumbled

⅛ teaspoon dried basil,
crumbled

⅛ teaspoon dried sage,
crumbled

⅛ teaspoon chopped fresh
tarragon

⅛ teaspoon chopped fresh
dill

1 pound fresh shrimp,
peeled and deveined

2 cups sliced fresh okra

1 cup fresh bay scallops

8 oysters, shucked, with
liquor

6 small clams in shells

½ cup chopped cooked
chicken

½ cup chopped fresh
ocean perch

½ cup flaked fresh
crabmeat

Melt bacon drippings in 5-quart
Dutch oven over medium heat.

Add flour and stir until copper color, about 15 minutes. Add onion, celery, green onion, green pepper, parsley and garlic and cook 1 hour, stirring frequently to prevent sticking.

Add stock, water, wine, tomatoes, catsup, bay leaf, filé powder, salt and herbs. Cook 1½ hours, stirring occasionally.

Blend in remaining ingredients. Cook 40 minutes. Discard bay leaf. Serve immediately.

Meat and Poultry Soups

Chinese Hot Pot Soup

Make this easy soup in minutes in the microwave.

Makes about 5½ cups

- ½ pound lean ground beef
- 2 14½-ounce cans beef stock
- 2¾ cups water
- 1 10-ounce package frozen Chinese stir-fry vegetables
- ½ cup instant rice
- ¼ cup sliced green onion
- 1 tablespoon soy sauce

Crumble beef into 1½-quart ovenproof glass baking dish.

Cook on High 1½ minutes. Crumble with fork and cook on High until browned, about 1½ minutes. Pour off fat. Add remaining ingredients. Cover and cook on High 10 minutes, stirring once or twice. Serve hot.

Meatball Soup with Escarole and Parsley Bread Squares

Makes 1 gallon

Chicken Stock
- 16 cups (1 gallon) water
- 1 2- to 3-pound chicken
- 1 small beef short rib
- 1 28-ounce can tomatoes
- 2 celery stalks, cut into pieces
- 1 onion, chopped
- 1 carrot, peeled
- 2 chicken bouillon cubes
- 1 beef bouillon cube
  Salt and freshly ground pepper

- 2 bunches escarole, washed and coarsely chopped

- 1½ pounds lean ground beef

¼ cup plus 1 tablespoon
       grated Parmesan cheese
½ teaspoon salt
½ teaspoon freshly ground
       pepper
 4 carrots, peeled and cut
       into thin rounds

 2 eggs
       Parsley Bread Squares*

Combine water, chicken, beef rib,
tomatoes, celery, onion, carrot,
bouillon cubes, salt and pepper
in large stockpot and bring to
boil over high heat. Reduce heat
and continue boiling 2 to 2½
hours, adding more water if
necessary. Let cool slightly.
Strain mixture through cheese-
cloth-lined strainer into large
bowl. Repeat. Skin chicken and
discard bones; chop meat or tear
into shreds. Set aside. Discard
beef rib and vegetables. Let broth
cool completely. Skim fat from
surface and discard.

Bring large saucepan of water to
rolling boil. Add escarole and
cook 5 minutes. Drain and pat
dry with paper towels.

Combine ground beef, ¼ cup
Parmesan, salt and pepper in

large bowl and mix well. Shape into 1-inch meatballs. Bring chicken broth to boil over medium heat. Add meatballs and cook 10 minutes. Stir in escarole and carrot rounds. Continue cooking 10 minutes.

Beat eggs with remaining 1 tablespoon Parmesan in small bowl. Add to boiling soup and continue cooking, stirring constantly with fork, 5 minutes. Remove from heat. Stir in chopped chicken and Parsley Bread Squares. Serve immediately.

*Parsley Bread Squares

    4 eggs
    ½ cup grated Parmesan cheese
    ¼ cup chopped fresh parsley
    ½ teaspoon salt
    ½ teaspoon freshly ground pepper
    ½ cup (or more) all purpose flour

    ¼ cup plus 1 tablespoon vegetable oil

Beat eggs, cheese, parsley, salt and pepper in large bowl until well blended. Add ½ cup flour one tablespoon at a time, mixing well after each addition (mixture should be thick; add more all purpose flour one teaspoon at a time, if necessary).

Heat oil in 10-inch nonstick (or heavy) skillet over high heat. Pour in batter, spreading to sides of skillet with spatula. Cook until browned on bottom, about 3 minutes. Turn over and continue cooking until browned, about 3 minutes. Transfer to paper towels and let cool. Cut bread into small squares.

Goulash Soup

6 servings

- 6 tablespoons solid vegetable shortening
- 2 medium onions, finely chopped
- 1 pound beef chuck, cut into ¾-inch cubes
- 3 tablespoons tomato paste
- 3 tablespoons paprika
- 1 tablespoon caraway seeds
- 1 garlic clove, crushed

1½ teaspoons dried
     marjoram, crumbled
  1 teaspoon finely grated
     lemon peel
     Dash of hot pepper
     sauce
     Pinch of sugar
  8 cups water
  2 small potatoes, peeled
     and cut into ¾-inch
     cubes
     Salt and freshly ground
     pepper

Melt 3 tablespoons shortening
in 8-quart stockpot over medium heat. Add chopped onion
and sauté until golden. Remove
stockpot from heat.

Melt remaining shortening in
large skillet over medium-high
heat. Add meat in batches and
brown well on all sides. Add to
onion. Pour small amount water
into skillet and stir up any
browned bits clinging to bottom. Blend into meat mixture.

Stir in tomato paste, paprika,
caraway seeds, garlic, marjoram, lemon peel, hot pepper
sauce and sugar. Add water and
mix well. Place over high heat
and bring to boil. Reduce heat,

cover partially and simmer 1½ hours. Add potatoes and continue cooking until potatoes are tender, about 20 minutes. Skim off fat. Season with salt and pepper. Ladle into bowls and serve.

Borscht

4 servings

1	raw beet, peeled and shredded
⅓	cup water
1	pound lean beef, cubed
3	cups beef stock
2	cups water
1½	teaspoons salt
½	cup coarsely grated carrot
½	cup coarsely grated turnip
1	small onion, chopped
2	tablespoons vinegar or to taste
1	tablespoon tomato paste
1	tablespoon butter
½	teaspoon sugar
1	16-ounce can sliced *or* shredded beets, drained (reserve juice)
1	cup shredded cabbage

1 bay leaf
   Freshly ground pepper
   Sour cream and fresh
   dill sprigs (garnishes)

Combine raw beet and water and let stand several hours.

Combine beef, stock, water and salt in large saucepan and simmer, skimming surface frequently, until meat is tender, about 1½ to 2 hours.

While meat is cooking, combine carrot, turnip, onion, vinegar, tomato paste, butter and sugar in small saucepan. Cover and simmer about 15 minutes, checking occasionally to be sure mixture isn't too dry. Add canned beet juice and cabbage and continue to cook 10 minutes.

When meat is tender, add vegetable mixture, canned beets, bay leaf and a few grindings of pepper and cook until heated through. Add undrained raw beet. Taste and adjust salt and vinegar as necessary. Discard bay leaf. Ladle soup into bowls and garnish with sour cream and dill. Serve immediately.

Cream of Reuben Soup

8 servings

- ½ cup beef stock
- ½ cup chicken stock
- ¼ cup coarsely chopped celery
- ¼ cup coarsely chopped onion
- ¼ cup coarsely chopped green bell pepper
- 1 tablespoon cornstarch dissolved in 2 tablespoons water
- 1 cup (about ¼ pound) coarsely chopped corned beef
- 1 cup chopped Swiss cheese
- ¾ cup sauerkraut, drained and rinsed

- ¼ cup (½ stick) butter
- 2 cups half and half
  Chopped fresh chives (garnish)

Combine first 5 ingredients in large saucepan and bring to boil over high heat. Reduce heat and simmer until vegetables are crisp-tender, about 5 minutes. Add dissolved cornstarch and continue cooking until soup thickens. Remove from heat and stir in corned beef, Swiss cheese and sauerkraut, blending well.

Melt butter in large double boiler over medium heat. Stir in half and half. Add soup and blend until smooth. Heat through but do not boil. Garnish with chives.

Bean and Sausage Chowder

6 servings

- ½ pound bacon
- 1 medium onion, chopped
- ½ cup chopped celery
- ⅓ cup chopped green bell pepper
- 2 tablespoons all purpose flour
- 2 16-ounce cans kidney beans
- 2 cups water
- ½ cup thinly sliced carrot
- 3 beef bouillon cubes
- 1 bay leaf
- ⅛ teaspoon freshly ground pepper
- 12 ounces fully cooked Polish sausage, thinly sliced

Fry bacon in heavy large skillet until crisp. Drain on paper towels. Crumble into bowl and set aside. Transfer 2 tablespoons bacon drippings to large saucepan. Add onion, celery and green pepper. Cover and cook over medium-high heat until tender, about 10 minutes. Remove from heat. Stir in flour, blending thoroughly. Add next 6 ingredients. Place over medium-high heat and bring to boil, stirring constantly. Reduce heat, cover and simmer 25 minutes. Add sausage, cover and continue simmering 10 minutes. Ladle chowder into bowls. Sprinkle with reserved bacon and serve immediately.

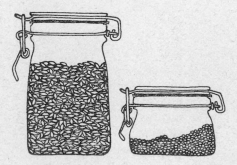

Sausage Garbure

Tradition dictates that you pour a splash of red wine from your glass into the garbure at the table.

2 servings

    3 cups water
    ¼ cup dried Great
       Northern *or* navy beans
    1 1-pound smoked ham
       hock
    1 small turnip, peeled and
       diced
    1 medium carrot, sliced
    1 medium celery stalk,
       sliced
    ½ small onion, sliced
    2 garlic cloves, minced
    1 parsley sprig
    ½ bay leaf
       Pinch *each* of dried
       marjoram, dried thyme
       and dried red pepper
       flakes
    ½ pound cabbage,
       shredded
    ½ cup peeled, diced boiling
       potato
    4 ounces kielbasa, chorizo
       or cotechino sausage

4 ounces fresh fava beans
   (about 4), shelled, *or* 1
   ounce shelled fava *or*
   lima beans
2 ounces fresh peas,
   shelled (2 to 3
   tablespoons)
   Salt and freshly ground
   pepper

   Croûtes*
2 tablespoons minced
   fresh parsley

Combine water and dried beans
in large saucepan and bring to
boil over high heat. Let boil 2
minutes. Remove from heat,
cover and let stand 1 hour (or
soak beans overnight without
boiling). Add ham hock, turnip,
carrot, celery, onion, garlic,
herbs and pepper flakes and
bring to boil. Reduce heat, cover
partially and simmer 45 minutes. Add cabbage and potato
and continue cooking until vegetables are tender, about 45
minutes. *(Can be prepared ahead
to this point and refrigerated.)*

Prick sausage in several places
with fork. Add to soup with fava
beans and peas and cook 30

minutes, adding more water if soup is too thick. Season to taste with salt and pepper.

To serve, remove ham hock and sausage. Discard bone and tendon from hock; cut meat into bite-size pieces. Cut sausage into long diagonal slices. Return meats to soup. Place 1 croûte in each heated bowl. Ladle soup over. Sprinkle with fresh parsley.

*Croûtes

    2 ¾- to 1-inch-thick slices
       French bread
    1 tablespoon olive oil

Preheat oven to 325°F. Arrange bread slices in single layer on baking sheet. Bake 15 minutes. Brush both sides with olive oil; turn slices over. Bake 15 minutes.

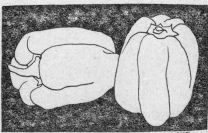

JEANNE

Spanish Sausage and Lentil Soup

This soup is even better when prepared 2 or 3 days ahead.

8 to 10 servings

- 2 tablespoons olive oil
- 1 pound chorizo *or* other spicy garlic sausage
- 7 ounces smoked ham, finely chopped
- 2 large onions, finely chopped
- 1 large green bell pepper, seeded and finely chopped
- 1 medium carrot, finely chopped
- 2 garlic cloves, minced
- 1 bay leaf
- ¾ teaspoon fresh thyme *or* ¼ teaspoon dried
- ½ teaspoon ground cumin

- 8 to 9 cups rich chicken stock (preferably homemade)
- 1 1-pound can peeled tomatoes
- ½ pound (1¼ cups) dried lentils

  Salt and freshly ground pepper

12 large spinach leaves,
washed, trimmed and
finely shredded

Heat olive oil in heavy 6- to 8-quart saucepan over medium heat. Add sausage and cook until almost all fat is rendered. Transfer sausage to platter. Drain off all but 2 tablespoons grease from saucepan. Add ham, onion, green pepper and carrot. Cover and cook 15 minutes, stirring occasionally. Stir in garlic, bay leaf, thyme and cumin. Cover and cook 5 minutes.

Meanwhile, cut sausage into thin slices. Add to saucepan with chicken stock, tomatoes and lentils. Reduce heat to low, cover partially and simmer gently until lentils begin to dissolve, about 2 hours. *(Can be prepared up to 3 days ahead and refrigerated, or frozen up to 3 months.)*

Discard any fat from surface. Remove bay leaf. Taste and adjust seasoning with salt and pepper. Simmer until just warmed through. Add shredded spinach. Transfer soup to tureen or individual bowls and serve.

Split Pea and Lentil Soup with Ham

Makes about 8 cups

- 1 2½-pound smoked picnic shoulder ham, trimmed
- 5 cups water
- 1 cup split peas
- 1 cup lentils

- 4 cups chicken stock (preferably homemade)
- 1 medium onion, chopped
- 1 medium carrot, chopped
- 1 medium celery stalk, chopped
- 1 large garlic clove, halved
- 1 small bay leaf
- ½ teaspoon sugar
- ⅛ teaspoon dried thyme, crumbled

   Salt and freshly ground pepper

Combine ham, 5 cups water, peas and lentils in stockpot. Bring to boil over high heat. Reduce heat to low, cover and simmer 1 hour, stirring occasionally.

Add 4 cups stock, onion, carrot, celery, garlic, bay leaf, sugar and thyme. Simmer uncovered over low heat 1 hour, stirring occasionally. Cool soup slightly.

Remove ham from bone and cut into ½-inch cubes. Discard garlic and bay leaf from soup. Remove vegetables with slotted spoon and push through coarse sieve to mash. Return ham and vegetables to soup. Simmer over low heat until thick, about 30 mintues. Season to taste with salt and pepper and serve.

Karwendel Soup

This satisfying Austrian soup is named for the mountain range of its origin.

4 servings

- 3 ounces (heaping ½ cup) diced lean bacon
- ¾ pound smoked Polish sausage (such as kielbasa) *or* other garlic pork sausage (casings removed if necessary), diagonally sliced ¾ inch thick
- 1 cup finely chopped onion

½ cup chopped carrot
½ cup chopped celery
1 1-pound can peeled
   tomatoes, coarsely
   chopped
2½ cups water
1 cup dried lentils, rinsed
   Salt and freshly ground
   pepper
½ teaspoon dried basil
¼ teaspoon dried
   marjoram
⅛ teaspoon sugar
1 large bay leaf
2 tablespoons finely
   chopped fresh parsley
   Dijon mustard *or*
   German-style mustard

Cook bacon in heavy kettle or Dutch oven over medium heat until golden but not crisp. Remove bacon from drippings and set aside. Pour off all but 1 tablespoon drippings from kettle. Add sausage and brown on all sides; remove, drain and set aside. Skim off excess fat.

Sauté onion, carrot and celery until onion is tender. Add tomatoes, water and lentils. Stir in reserved bacon and sausage, salt and pepper, basil, marjoram, sugar and bay leaf. Cover and simmer until lentils are tender, about 1 hour, stirring occasionally. Taste and adjust seasoning with salt and pepper. Discard bay leaf. Ladle into soup plates. Sprinkle with parsley. Dab mustard on sausages if desired.

Goulash Soup with Sauerkraut

This soup mellows and improves in flavor if prepared a day in advance.

6 to 8 servings

> 1 tablespoon vegetable oil
> 1½ to 2 pounds lean pork, cut into ½-inch cubes
>
> 3 to 4 tablespoons butter *or* lard
> 4 large onions, finely chopped
> 4 carrots, finely chopped
> 2 celery stalks, finely chopped
> 1 large garlic clove, minced
> 2 to 3 tablespoons Hungarian sweet paprika

1½ teaspoons fresh thyme
   or ½ teaspoon dried
1½ teaspoons fresh savory
   or ½ teaspoon dried
¼ teaspoon whole caraway
   seeds
2½ to 3 quarts beef stock
   (preferably homemade)
2 cups canned tomatoes in
   puree
1 cup chopped cabbage
1 pound sauerkraut,
   rinsed and drained
2 large potatoes, peeled
   and cut into small cubes
   Salt and freshly ground
   pepper
   Sour cream (optional
   garnish)

Preheat broiler. Lightly coat shallow baking pan with 1 tablespoon oil. Add pork in single layer. Broil quickly until well browned on all sides. Drain thoroughly on paper towels.

Melt butter or lard in 6- to 8-quart saucepan over medium-high heat. Add onion, carrots and celery and cook until onion begins to brown. Stir in pork, garlic, paprika, thyme, savory and caraway. Add stock, tomatoes and cabbage. Reduce heat, cover partially and simmer about 1½ hours. Stir in sauerkraut and simmer 30 minutes. Add potatoes and simmer another 30 minutes. Season with salt and pepper. Transfer soup to tureen or individual bowls. Serve immediately. Garnish with dollop of sour cream if desired.

China Honey Pork and Greens

This soup should be served with individual bowls of additional rice.

6 servings

- 1 3-pound boneless pork shoulder blade *or* butt (about 3½ pounds before boning and tying)
- 3 tablespoons honey

- 2 tablespoons peanut oil
- 6 cups cold water
- 1 cup dry white wine
- 3 tablespoons sugar
- ⅛ teaspoon dried red pepper flakes
- ¼ cup soy sauce

½ teaspoon freshly ground white pepper

3 pounds bok choy
1½ cups hot steamed rice
Soy sauce
Freshly ground white pepper

Place meat in heavy large kettle or Dutch oven and cover with cold water. Heat to boiling, then cover and simmer 1 hour. Drain off water and dry meat. Rub pork roast thoroughly with honey.

Heat oil in kettle over medium heat. Add meat and brown well on all sides. Add water, wine, sugar, red pepper flakes, ¼ cup soy sauce and white pepper. Cover tightly and simmer until meat is very tender, about 2 hours, turning occasionally. Place meat on plate and remove strings. Keep meat warm.

Trim off and discard solid ends of cabbage. Cut remaining cabbage (about 2 pounds) crosswise, slicing tender top portions into 1½-inch pieces and heavy lower portions into 1-inch pieces. Heat liquid in kettle to boiling. Add greens and cook just until tender, about 5 to 10 minutes. Serve portion of meat, some greens, spoonful of rice and ladle of broth in each soup bowl. Pass additional soy sauce and white pepper.

Hot and Sour Soup

Serve with a crisp Pilsner-style beer or Chinese beer.

6 servings

>   15 dried tiger lily buds*
>   5 dried black Chinese mushrooms*
>   1 tablespoon dried cloud ear mushrooms*
>
>   7 to 8 cups rich chicken stock
>   ⅓ cup shredded winter bamboo shoots*
>   ½ cup thinly sliced water chestnuts
>   6 ounces lean pork, finely shredded
>   4 teaspoons soy sauce
>   1 20-ounce package tofu, rinsed and cut into ½-inch dice

*Available at oriental markets.

1 cup shredded cooked chicken

3 to 5 tablespoons distilled white vinegar

2 to 3 teaspoons freshly ground pepper

2 tablespoons cornstarch mixed with 3 tablespoons water

1 egg, lightly beaten

1 large green onion, minced (garnish)

Dash of sesame oil, or to taste

Place tiger lily buds, Chinese mushrooms and cloud ears in separate small bowls and add enough hot water to cover. Soak until softened, about 30 minutes. Drain each. Set buds aside. Discard hard centers from cloud ears, then slice remainder into julienne. Remove stems from mushrooms (reserve for later use) and slice caps into julienne.

Combine buds, black mushrooms, cloud ears, chicken stock, bamboo shoots, water chestnuts, pork and soy sauce in 5- to 6-quart stockpot and bring to simmer over medium heat. Reduce heat, cover and

cook 4 minutes. Add tofu,
chicken, vinegar and pepper.
Blend in cornstarch mixture and
simmer until soup thickens
slightly. Stir in beaten egg.
Transfer soup to tureen or individual bowls. Sprinkle with
green onion and sesame oil to
taste and serve.

Guamanian Hot and Sour Soup

6 servings

- 1 quart chicken stock
- ½ cup canned bamboo
  shoots, rinsed, drained
  and thinly sliced
- ¼ cup cooked shredded
  pork or beef
- 1 tablespoon soy sauce
- 7 ounces bean curd, rinsed
  and cut into ½-inch dice
- 2 tablespoons distilled
  white vinegar
- ¼ teaspoon freshly ground
  pepper
- 3 tablespoons cornstarch
- 3 tablespoons water
- 1 egg, beaten to blend
- 2 teaspoons sesame oil

1 teaspoon dried red
   pepper flakes
1 medium green onion,
   finely chopped

Combine chicken stock, bamboo shoots, pork and soy sauce in heavy Dutch oven. Bring to boil over high heat. Reduce heat to low, cover and simmer 3 minutes. Add bean curd, vinegar and pepper. Return to boil over low heat. Mix cornstarch and water in small bowl and stir into soup. Slowly stir in egg. Remove from heat and blend in sesame oil and red pepper flakes. Ladle into bowls. Garnish with chopped green onion and serve.

Ajiaco

Allow guests to add the condiments to their own dishes according to their tastes.

6 servings

   1 5-pound roasting chicken, cut into serving pieces
   1 celery stalk with leaves
   1 large onion, peeled and quartered
   2 bay leaves
   1 large parsley sprig
   4 tablespoons ground cumin
   2 teaspoons salt
   ¼ teaspoon freshly ground pepper
   6 medium potatoes, peeled and quartered

   6 ears fresh corn
   3 ripe avocados, scooped into balls
   1 cup whipping cream
   ½ cup drained capers
   4 hard-cooked eggs, chopped
     Aji Sauce*

Cover chicken with cold water. Bring to boil and simmer 5 minutes. Drain liquid and rinse chicken pieces. Return chicken to kettle with 6 cups cold water, celery, onion, bay leaves, parsley, cumin, salt, pepper and 4 potatoes. Cover, bring to boil and simmer until chicken is tender, about 45 to 60 minutes.

With slotted spoon, remove chicken and potatoes from broth. Strain broth, removing excess fat from top. Return broth to kettle. Mash cooked potatoes and stir into broth. Skin and bone chicken, leaving meat in large pieces. Add uncooked potatoes to broth. Cover and cook until potatoes are just tender, about 15 minutes.

Cut kernels from 3 ears of corn. Slice remaining corn crosswise into pieces 2 inches thick. When potatoes are tender, add chicken and all corn to broth. Cook just until corn is tender, about 5 minutes. Taste and correct seasoning with cumin, salt and pepper. Remove bay leaves. Ladle into wide soup plates, placing a piece of corn and a piece of potato in each. Serve avocado balls on the side. Pass pitcher of cream and bowls of capers, eggs and Aji Sauce separately.

*Aji Sauce

- 6 tablespoons very finely chopped fresh cilantro
- ½ cup olive oil
- 2 tablespoons minced green onion (white part only)
- 1½ tablespoons fresh lemon juice
- 2 teaspoons finely chopped fresh parsley
- 1 teaspoon white wine vinegar
- ½ teaspoon (or more) crushed dried red pepper flakes
- ½ teaspoon salt
- ¼ teaspoon freshly ground pepper, or to taste

Combine all ingredients and mix thoroughly with a fork.

Turkey Vegetable Soup

6 to 8 servings

- ¼ cup (½ stick) butter or margarine
- 2 medium onions, chopped
- 2 tablespoons all purpose flour
- 1 teaspoon curry powder
- 3 cups chicken broth
- 1 cup chopped potatoes
- ½ cup thinly sliced carrots
- ½ cup sliced celery
- 2 tablespoons chopped fresh parsley
- ½ teaspoons sage or poultry seasoning
- 2 cups cubed cooked turkey
- 1½ cups half and half
- 1 10-ounce package frozen chopped spinach
  Salt and freshly ground pepper

Melt butter in large saucepan over medium-high heat. Add onion and sauté until translucent, about 10 minutes. Stir in flour and curry powder and cook 2 to 3 minutes. Add broth, potatoes, carrots, celery, parsley and sage and bring to boil. Reduce heat to low, cover and simmer 10 minutes. Add turkey, half and half and spinach. Cover and continue simmering until heated through, about 7 minutes. Season with salt and pepper. Serve hot.

Index

Credits

The following people contributed the recipes included in this book:

Terrie Achacoso
Beethoven Restaurant, San Francisco, California
Adrienne Blocker
Charles Royce Bridges
Sharon Cadwallader
Sue Cam
Elyn and Phil Clarkson
Elizabeth Colchie
Shirley Collins
Terry Flettrich
Freddi Greenberg
Connie Grigsby
Betsy Harker
Jim and Linda Jenkins
John Nero Restaurant, Green Bay, Wisconsin
Barbara Karoff
Lynne Kasper
Marlene Kellner
Barby Lages
Abby Mandel
Amy Marchand
Perla Meyers
Charles Mincks
Jefferson and Jinx Morgan
Shelley Oberholser
Judith Olert
Judith Olney
Joan Robinson
Marilyn Sandonato
Shirley Sarvis
Renee Simmons
Miriam Sinclair

92 Hearty Soups

Lee Standen
Elaine Wally
Marty Westerman
Val White
Sheila Wild